PRISTINE DROPS OF DEW

LATHA PRAKASH

I dedicate this book to my parents.

Thank you for always believing in me.

A special thank you to my always encouraging sister-in-law who believed in me and suggested that I publish a book.

I dedicate this book to my husband who is my constant support.

I dedicate this book to my parents-in-law and my family.

Contents

Contents

Contents

Foreword

When Dr. Latha Prakash revealed to me that she is all set to add another feather to her hat -the idea to compile all her stories into a book "Pristine Drops of Dew", I was overjoyed as I knew that this was coming. Thereafter, when she contacted me to put together a foreword for her debut novella, I was humbled. Thank you, Latha, for keeping me in your thoughts.

Latha's first book "Pristine Drops of Dew" is unputdownable. It's a compilation of well-curated stories stitched with some humor, adventure, mystery, and romance.

Briefly put, "Pristine Drops of Dew" is an anthology of stories to entertain, distract, reassure and inspire – just what a short story should do.

Chanpreet Kaur Sethi
Content Strategist @ www.momspresso.com

Preface

I'm a dentist by profession and a bibliophile by choice. Books are my comfort place. A couple of years back when the nationwide lockdown was announced, I took my first baby step into the world of writing and began to unravel its beauty.

I gave wings to my imagination and set my soul free. I let my thoughts meander and my pen take its course.

My husband, my parents and my family became the wind beneath my wings, motivating me to give form to my thoughts.

My husband became my driving force and I began to explore the world of fiction. I ventured to write fantasy tales, romantic stories, heart-warming, inspirational and moral oriented stories.

This book is my humble and maiden compilation of short stories. While most of them are in the 100 word format, a few have exceeded the word limit.

This is just the beginning and I have a long way to go. I have myriad things to learn and Miles to cover.

The book is interspersed with few surprises for the readers. Make sure to read the book completely.

Hope you enjoy the reading experience.

Acknowledgements

I would like to thank my parents for always believing in me. I would like to thank my husband for his incessant and unwavering support. I would like to thank my family for supporting me in this beautiful journey and appreciating every small and big effort I made.

A special thanks to my cousin for introducing me to Momspreesso.

Also, I would like to express my gratitude to Momspresso for providing me with a platform to begin my writing journey and share my thoughts. I would like to thank Chanpreet Kaur Sethi for her guidance.

Last but not the least, I would like to thank all my blogger friends and readers for encouraging me with their valuable feedback.

My heartfelt gratitude to God for instilling faith and self-belief within me and standing by my side in every walk of life.

This is just the beginning and I have leaves to unravel and stones to turn as I continue my journey in the world of writing.

Prologue

What comes to your mind when you come across a word or look at a picture? Does it make you think? Does it stir myriad emotions within you? Do you wish to paint? Well, when I come across a word or group of words, I wish to weave a story around them. Each picture conveys a unique story that needs to be unravelled.

That is how this book came into being. Every morning Momspresso challenges us with a word and I accomplish the task by weaving a story around it.

Turn the leaves of this book to feel the spell that the words cast on you.

CHAPTER ONE

Do You Have A Skeleton In Your Closet?

I haven't told anyone.
Can you keep this a secret?
I have heard people telling this to me at intervals frequent,
"If it is a secret, then why divulge it in the first place?"
I wondered aloud,
A secret must be preserved in the nook of the heart and not be announced, I frowned,
Instead of worrying about the credibility of your secret keeper,
Stop disclosing the skeleton in your closet,
Take your inner self into confidence,
Stop depending on others,
Be your own trusted companion and
Live a peaceful and happy life.

CHAPTER TWO

You Are Under Arrest

Adjusting her saree and tucking her loose tresses inside the bun,

Preeti scurried around the house mentally making note of every minute detail.

Suddenly, someone tugged her into a dim-lit corner.

"You had given me a slip this morning. Don't try to escape from my grasp now," she heard a voice. "I wish to remain in the custody of your embrace till eternity," she replied her cheeks turning pink. His cheeks showed a tinge of pink too as his hands enveloped her waist like a waistband. While the rest of the family were busy in the festive preparations, the quinquagenarian couple seized every opportunity, dim or bright to spend some private moments.

CHAPTER THREE

Don't Say Yes When You Want To Say No

On the days you feel low,
When every fibre in you wants to say a stern no,
Don't say yes and
Make your life a mess,
When you can't help,
Just politely deny and
Your opinion you firmly imply,
Fret not about letting others down,
In response to your No,
Many may frown,
Stay calm and sit back on your throne,
Adjust your imaginary crown,
Never go on a guilt trip just because you denied to
assist your near and dear,
You had just made your point of view clear,
But in the process, be prepared to hear a blanket denial,
As yes and no are a part of one's life cycle.

CHAPTER FOUR

You Filled Our Lives With Light

Basking in the moonlight and
Holding onto the glimmer of hope,
I paced up and down the corridor anxiously,
With my gaze fixated on the sliding doors,
On which the words Restricted Area was printed in bold and red,
An hour passed in dreary anticipation,
Suddenly, I heard a low shrill cry,
I turned and observed that a nurse rushed out of the room,
"Congratulations, it's a girl," she said,
Tears of joy cascaded down my cheeks,
While my lips parted into a wide smile.
After losing a child and giving birth to a stillborn,
You entered our lives filling them with light.
The moment I carried you in my arms,
While fondly stroking your mother's hair,
Is A Moment Without A Dimension,
That would be preserved in the treasure trove of memories forever.

CHAPTER FIVE

Past Life, Does It Matter

My love for tranquil waters makes me wonder,
If in my last birth I was an elegant fish,
I can't help ponder if in my last birth,
I was an alluring bird for my urge to fly free in the vast azure sky is not a secret,
My 'Never Give Up' attitude makes me think,
If in my last birth I was an achiever,
What was I?
A doer or just a hinderer,
As I strolled in the park perturbed,
It occurred to me that the past is in the past,
It doesn't matter who I was in my last birth,
What I am going to do during this life span,
Is what matters,
I would love to explore the unruffled waters,
Flying high and touching the blanket of stars would give me an adrenaline rush,
By fulfilling every dream of mine whether small or big,
I want to live a happy, peaceful and efficacious life.

CHAPTER SIX

Their Covert Operation

The pale crescent moon shone in the night sky,
Sheila and her neighbour Seema served their families early dinner,
Making sure that their family members were fast asleep,
The women surreptitiously walked out of their respective houses,
As the dogs barked at a distance breaking the night's silence,
Their feet enjoyed the touch of the copious, velvety sand on the seashore,
Suddenly, wings emerged from Seema's shoulder blades,
While fins made an appearance from either side of
Sheila's waist, Sheila dove deep into the water and
Took a tour of the colourful coral reefs accompanied by eels, tunas and dolphins,
Seema enjoyed her little jaunt in the vast sky,
After an hour, the women were back on the sand rejuvenated and full of vigour,
Exchanging warm smiles, the coral woman and the
empyrean woman walked back to their homes,
Promising to keep their little secret intact.

CHAPTER SEVEN

A Merry Christmas For Us

After manoeuvring through the city's traffic,
I reached home late in the evening,
Lining the exterior of the house were palm trees that were decorated with lights,
The bedazzled house left me pleasantly surprised,
In the corner of our humble abode,
A Christmas tree decorated with beautiful dolls,
lanterns gave me a warm welcome,
I walked towards it and
Found a piece of paper with the words 'Look Within' written on it that was attached to the stockings,
My eyes misted as I saw the pregnancy kit with two pink lines,
'A wish come true,' I thought as I observed my wife gazing at me,
Leaving my office bag on the floor, I ran to her, hugged her tightly,
Lifted her in my arms and twirled her in the air,
This Christmas was indeed happy for us.

CHAPTER EIGHT

The Jingle That Filled A Heart With Happiness

The window chime swayed in the direction of the breeze, creating a pleasant jingle. Smile embraced Rajeev's lips. As he tossed and turned on the bed, his hands curled around Priya's waist and dragged her onto the bed. As his lips took a tour of her vivacious curves, he could feel her blush.

"How did you know it was me?" asked Priya.

"The cheerful jingle produced by your bangles and the alluring aroma of your perfume convey to me about your presence. I may not be able to get a glimpse of your bangles but they fill my otherwise dark life with colours," explained Rajeev.

Wrapping her arms around him she slipped into a utopian world one more time.

CHAPTER NINE

When Life Plays The Trumpet

Waking up to the blaring sound of the trumpet on the television, twelve-year-old Nimisha stomped out of her room. As she watched the actress on the television walk with panache, pictures of a little girl welcomed by Trumpet Calls and a shower of flowers while she wielded her sword at lightning speed flashed before her eyes. The sense of deja vu made her mind hazy.

Clasping her dizzy head, "Hail the warrior princess Vanika" she announced with one hand on her hips and the other hand waving in the air.

While the rest of her family looked at her perplexed, the nonagenarian house help turned family member Meenakshi amma's eyes twinkled in joy. Her face gleamed and heart somersaulted and 'The dauntless princess Vanika Rajput has resurrected as Nimisha,' she thought with tears rolling in her eyes.

CHAPTER TEN

Her Life Revolves Around HER

Seated at the dining table Meena began to peel the potatoes. "I'm planning to make potato fry for lunch," she announced. But all she got in response was stark silence. She looked around and found no one. The truth stung her like a bee. Her only daughter Rupa was married six months back and she has been a empty nester since then. Closing her eyes she imagined Rupa's eyes widen on hearing the word potato fry. Meena's lips parted into a wry smile. Keeping the potatoes aside she decided to make brinjal for lunch. Pictures of Rupa's flared nostrils at the mere mention of brinjal flashed before her. Meena's life revolved around Rupa even when she wasn't around her.

CHAPTER ELEVEN

Hum Nahi Sudhrenge

As I sat scanning the newspaper, the doorbell rang. My wife Sirisha marched towards the door and opened it. I observed that a delivery boy was standing in the doorway holding a big sized bag in his hands. Sirisha thanked him and walked into the kitchen, clutching the bag close to her chest. She began to empty the bag while I sat trying to pry into the contents. Looking at me, she grinned widely.

That innocent countenance and enchanting smile stirred suspicion in my heart. I knew she was up to something but couldn't decipher her intentions. The situation demanded that I did a thorough investigation.

Springing out of the couch, I entered the kitchen and asked, "What is going on wifey?"
"Oh, it's nothing," she tried to dodge answering my question.
"You are no less than Hercules Poirot," I told myself. After fifteen minutes of incessant questioning, she finally gave in. My grit and perseverance won and I was about to jump in joy but her revelation poured cold water over my victory.

"I am planning to make rumali roti," she said. My heart

almost stopped beating but what she said next was unthinkable.
"I want you to shoot a video of the procedure and I will post the vlog on my social media pages later after editing it," she said her voice brimming with confidence.
I stood racking my brain for a solution and came up with an idea.

"Let's order food from our favourite restaurant. Sundays are meant for relaxation," I suggested.
But she was hell-bent on continuing with her plan and I had no option but to oblige.

After an hour of groundwork, everything was set for the mission. Images of our previous failures came cascading in front of my eyes. Chocolate cake, pizza and other delicacies turned out to be a disappointment.

Sirisha gave me her phone. The camera was on, everything was set. She began to knead the dough. After thirty minutes, she stood rolling a small portion of it. She placed the cauldron upside down on the stove. It was going smoothly and I was about to sigh in relief. But something unpredictable happened.

The roti got stuck to the cauldron and it transformed into papad. She tried to remove it but in the process, the cauldron fell on the floor and the kitchen was filled with smoke. I left the phone on the table and helped her in cleaning the kitchen. An hour passed in cleaning and crying over spilt milk.

I ordered our favourite pizza to cheer her up while she sat

reminiscing her failed attempts. We devoured the pizza and it gave her solace. Suddenly, her phone rang. She answered it and sank to the floor."Is everything okay?" I asked.

She informed me that the video I recorded got posted in the family group. I looked at her perplexed.

"Oh, it was my fault. I shared the wrong video by mistake," she said.

Our phones were bombarded with messages. We had become the butt of everyone's jokes. We sat reading the messages and burst into laughter while reminiscing our epic failure.

CHAPTER TWELVE

The Emotional Roller Coaster

The night before her wedding Preeti took a full view of the house she had painstakingly transformed into a home. She scanned every nook of her humble nest and myriad emotions churned in her heart. Tears gushed out of her eyes. Clearing her vision she tiptoed to the other room and observed that she was sleeping peacefully like a baby. He sat on the rocking chair flipping the leaves of the photo album, Preeti stealthily entered the room and placed her head on his lap. He affectionately stroked her hair. They had obliterated the suffix with ease and were all set to perform the kanyaadaan of their daughter-in-law turned daughter the next day.

CHAPTER THIRTEEN

Suno Mera Chiraag

My dear son,
Get into the kitchen,
Let's have some fun,
Assist your sister and me in cooking the festive meal,
To learn something new don't you have the zeal,
You boast of navigating through the city's traffic with ease,
While manoeuvring the three-burner stove please don't freeze,
Cooking isn't just a woman's job,
It is an essential life skill,
So just learn how to mop and chop,
As I speak my eyes mist,
Fondly I stroke my daughter's hair,
It was she who brought this change within me,
I'm in love with this updated version of myself, you see.

CHAPTER FOURTEEN

Adding Spice To Life

On some days I work at lightning speed completing every chore in a trice,
On the others,
I work at a snail's pace giving a tough competition to the tortoise,
On some days, I cook spicy and flavoursome delicacies,
While on the other days I cook bland food and label it as healthy,
While on some days I use every minute of my day prudently,
I while away time doing nothing on the others,
By changing my daily routine now and then,
I add spice to my otherwise mundane life,
After all, variety is the spice of life, isn't it?

CHAPTER FIFTEEN

The Hamara Bajaj

As I strolled in the garden,
Soaking in the fresh breeze,
My hair caressing my face,
My eyes fell on a little girl enjoying the motorbike ride with her father,
I closed my eyes and was transported to my childhood days,
Pictures of me hopping onto my dad's scooter,
Standing in the front and holding the handle flashed before me,
From picking me up from school to a worrisome ride to the paediatrician,
The fun ride to the park and theatre,
Our 'bajaj' scooter has been a witness to my blissful childhood,
Proving to be hamara bajaj in true spirit.

CHAPTER SIXTEEN

Clouds That Acted As A Guide

The blazing afternoon sun shone in the blue sky. As she rolled the dough she heard her baby coo. She turned and looked at her new-born with love-filled eyes. She then shifted her gaze to the offer letter on the table. Her mind was overcast, muddled between the choices.

Suddenly clouds formed in the afternoon sky. Within a few minutes, they burst and the city was drenched in rain. 'I'll focus on my career and be a good mom too. The darkest clouds precede the loveliest rains,' she thought smiling. The afternoon clouds had freed her of her tribulations.

CHAPTER SEVENTEEN

The Two Little Hands

"It only took five seconds to soil the clean kitchen," she yelled. Her little one turned and looked at her innocently, glistening tears running down her cheeks. "Why didn't you ask me if you wanted something?" she yelled. "You were suffering from a headache and I wanted to make coffee for you," replied her daughter. Her exasperation melted like snow. She hugged her daughter tightly and landed a kiss on her cheeks. It only took five seconds for the little munchkin to make her mother fall in love with her all over again.

CHAPTER EIGHTEEN

Survival Of The Fittest

A sprinting event was organised. As the participants braced themselves, the emperor announced, "The participant who reaches the finish line last will have his head cut off," leaving the participants shocked. The conch blew and the royal tournament began. The spectators cheered for their favourite contestant. The onlookers observed that the participants ran at breakneck speed. They ran not to win the contest but in an attempt to save their lives. 'Only the ones who emerge victoriously under adverse conditions will be a part of my army. It is all about the survival of the fittest,' thought the emperor smiling.

CHAPTER NINETEEN

The Humble Yet Important Element

Clad in a blue saree that complimented her slender waist with exquisite jewellery embracing her graciously, Sania looked alluring. Convinced of her dazzling persona, she sanguinely walked into the living room. Catching a glimpse of her from head to toe, "You look magnificent but something is missing," remarked her husband.

Her eyebrows arched into a question mark. She walked into the room and gazed at her reflection. While she was engrossed in looking for the missing element, her husband walked in and said, "You forgot your smile." She smiled on hearing that. "You are now complete," he said.

CHAPTER TWENTY

Is Clarity Everything?

'Clear thoughts, clear vision, an organised life,' this was my mantra,
I strived to steer clear of every confusion,
'Clarity about my future' was all that mattered,
When the pandemic started and dark clouds loomed over,
I was gripped by fear and confusion and
Life went for a toss,
HE once again proved who is the boss,
I learned the importance of living in the moment and
Expressing gratitude for every blessing I was bestowed with,
I stopped planning and started enjoying the impromptu situations,
Finally, I obtained clarity about the priorities of life,
Vagueness is bliss sometimes, isn't it?

CHAPTER TWENTY-ONE

Nayi Shuruaat Mubarak Ho

Accompanied by her father, Shweta entered her maternal home. The house was engulfed by darkness. 'I have brought disgrace to the family. Amma must be angry with me,' she thought. Suddenly, the living room lit up and her eyes fell on a cake. She walked to the centre table and found that CANDLES representing number twenty-three was arranged on the cake. "I'm twenty-five now," she muttered. "Forget the two years you had spent in hell. It's time you move on. Happy new beginnings beta," said her mother. SHE HAD HAPPY TEARS IN HER EYES as she cut the cake.

CHAPTER TWENTY-TWO

Choice, What's That?

The sun painted the sky in hues of orange. The branches swayed in synchronisation with the breeze. The birds were on their way back to their nests. The aroma of the incense sticks filled the air. The sound of the temple bells that rang in a distance filled everyone with positive vibes.

Under a huge tree, she sat on the banks of her namesake river Ganga. Babbling and burbling the river made its way over the rocks. The water shimmered like pearls under the slanting rays of the sun. Twigs twirled on its streaming surface. The enticing aroma of the river and the pleasant environment filled her soul with tranquillity.

"It is dadi's birthday. Let's celebrate it as per her choice," her grandson Raman's voice echoed in her ears. A pleasant smile embraced her lips that spread to the wrinkles in the corner of her eyes. After a few seconds, the smile was replaced with a grimace. Choice, the word seemed alien to her. In an attempt to be a good daughter, a dutiful wife, a caring daughter-in-law and a doting mother she had locked her dreams and choices in an unused corner of her heart.

She was married to the groom of her father's choice. A layer of vermilion at the parting of her hair and a mangalsutra worth a few thousands changed her life forever. Her husband didn't know what the word consent meant. Her choice never mattered to him. He was the centre of his life and his life revolved around himself.

Albeit her life was filled with material possessions there was a dearth of love and affection. She wanted her husband's attention and wished he had an iota of respect for her. But she always ended up disappointed. After a few years, she gave up her expectations.

Two years after marriage she embraced motherhood. Her dreams, aspiration and wishes got submerged under the mountain of responsibilities. Her family rarely remembered her birthday and even if they did she prepared their favourite delicacies. Not that her sons didn't love her. But they never realised that she may have her own opinion or choice.

Thinking back now she doesn't remember when was the last time she had her favourite food. What was her favourite colour? What was her favourite passtime? She doesn't remember. Nobody asked her what she wanted nor did she ever express.

Not just her family, her body too didn't respect her choices. She was diagnosed with cancer a year back and the cancer cells have metastasized to almost every organ of her body eating away the life within her.

"You have just a month left," she remembered the doctor's words. She reached for her bag and removed a writing pad and pen. She let the words flow and the characters take their course. She cherished the time spent on the banks of the river in the company of her pen and paper.

The time she spent writing was the only time when she followed her heart. She chose the genre of her choice and let the words flow. She never thought about publishing her stories but secretly wished that someday her words of wisdom would be cherished by her grandchildren.

After contemplating the title for her anthology she scribbled a few words on the paper. It read "Ganga's choice".

Looking at the river she wondered if the river Ganga had ever exercised her choice. The river filled with contaminants spoke for itself.

A few hours passed

Raman was busy searching for her. "Dadi," he shrieked as he descended the stairs. But she didn't respond.

Clasping the writing pad with one hand and the other hand immersed in the river Ganga lay her lifeless body. She finally breathed her last. Unfortunately, death too didn't knock on her door as per her choice.

CHAPTER TWENTY-THREE

Determination Gone With The Wind

Wiping off the droplets of sweat dancing on my forehead I walked to the refrigerator smiling all the way. These tiny droplets were not as a result of slogging in the kitchen. But I had earned those after an hour of cardio and strength training. As I opened the refrigerator a tiny box in the corner garnered my attention. My eyes widened and heart fluttered, but the mind immediately took the reins of self control in its hands. A few hours passed and there I was seated comfortably on the couch enjoying every drop of my favorite butterscotch icecream. Who knew my resolve firm like iron could be easily melted by this heavenly ambrosia?

CHAPTER TWENTY-FOUR

A Reflection That Led To Change

Tying the shoe lace tight,
She began to run with all her might,
Sweat dripped off her face,
Ignoring it she tried to maintain her pace,
After an hour of her morning exercise,
She reached home weary yet joyful to be concise,
Walking into her room she stared at her reflection,
Caressing her paunch she remembered her previous day's contemplation,
'My well being is of utmost priority,' she ascertained,
"Holding onto A bouquet of my reflections I will eliminate the myths around womanhood in my brain that are ingrained," she announced,
She began to take baby steps towards prioritizing herself.

CHAPTER TWENTY-FIVE

Your Life Jacket Lies Within You

When life throws gruesome challenges at you,
Shooting at you curveballs new,
Look at your reflection,
Hold your chin up and
Tell yourself, "I will do it. I will emerge victoriously this time too",
Remember your present is just a situation and
Not your final destination,
No matter how tangled your life is,
You posses the caliber to entangle it,
Give yourself a pep talk,
Start your day with positive affirmations,
'Cause these minor initiatives,
Will serve as a Life Jacket and
Prevent you from drowning in,
The rabbit hole of apathy, self-doubt and self-pity.

CHAPTER TWENTY-SIX

Who Is The Boss?

The Varma family clung to their seats engrossed in watching a movie. After making sure that everyone's eyes were fixated on the screen, Rajani Varma left the living room and stealthily crept into the kitchen.She grabbed a tin that was hidden behind the other utensils. Her eyes shone as she looked at those spongy, brunette balls. She picked one Gulab Jamun and was about to gobble it when she heard a clicking sound. Glancing sideways, she observed that Mr Varma was standing by her side.

"Pictures of your conspiracy are going to go viral," he grinned. Grabbing his collar, she pulled him closer and locked his lips with hers. Their romantic life had hit a dry spell and the kiss served as rain to the parched souls. While he was revelling in the magic, she furtively grabbed his phone and deleted the photographs. She was the boss after all and no one could ever mess with her.

CHAPTER TWENTY-SEVEN

A Beautiful And Pure Feeling

Making sure that even the tiniest ray of light wasn't falling on her, Divya stood in a dark corner of the hall witnessing the ceremony.

One by one every woman in the hall approached the would-be mother and slid bangles onto her hands and blessed her.

Divya yearned to bless her sister and the baby but her aunt had forbidden her from being a part of the ceremony.

She was tagged 'childless' and 'inauspicious'. Emotions rose and fell within her like the tides in the sea.

Tears that were confined within her eyes now cascaded freely down her cheeks. She couldn't bear a child.

But she still was a mother. A mother who took care of her baby sister when they lost their parents. A mother who cared for the well being of her friends and family.

A mother who was empathetic to all the living beings. Being a mother isn't only about passing on one's genes to the next generation.

It is an emotion. Maa is a feeling. A beautiful and pure one. Superstitions that limit this pristine emotion must not be condoned."

CHAPTER TWENTY-EIGHT

The Reunion In Their Haven

The fluffy clouds drifted lazily in the blue sky. Flapping their wings, the birds were taking a tour of the sky. Sheetal sat on a bench and her weary eyes made a note of the scene. Her gaze shifted to the sky.She could picture a lanky figure on the clouds. The lanky figure flashed a smile filled with love and assurance. A strange warmth enveloped her heart. Soon, another young form joined the lanky one. It appeared as though the two forms were engrossed in a discussion.Suddenly, they looked at Sheetal and waved at her. She looked at the sky and smiled wryly. Her husband had left the world a decade back and their son too had left her and joined his father a few months back. Tears rolled in her eyes as she stared at them. Carrying her wobbly self, she began to walk, waiting to reunite with her family, in their haven the 'heaven'.

CHAPTER TWENTY-NINE

Strike A Balance

You give undivided attention,
You give care and affection,
You give love without any expectations,
You give your time,
You give your energy,
You give a part of yourself,
You are a natural giver,
Pause for a second and reflect,
You have been giving your entire life,
Dear women, it's time you strike a balance and
Take time for yourself,
Take time to do something you love,
Take time to focus on your inner self,
You have been an adept manager in the lives of others,
It's time you be a good manager of your life,
You give so effortlessly,
So start taking without an ounce of guilt.

CHAPTER THIRTY

Shouldn't I Have My Share Of Argh Moments?

After ringing the doorbell for the tenth time in a row I stood waiting in the doorway while fidgeting with my phone impatiently. I was about to bang on the door angrily when the door opened and I was ushered inside.

Plastering a fake smile on my face I darted to the kitchen. Deep within my heart, I was cursing them for wasting my precious time. Every minute counts not just for them but for me too.

The sight of the sink filled with grimy vessels made me feel nauseous. Every spoon, bowl and ladle lay in the sink waiting to be fondly caressed by me.
'These people don't even wash their plates and spoons. What will they do without me?' I thought rolling my eyes and determinedly evading the Argh moment.

Diving my hands deep into the sink, I began to clean the

utensils at rocket speed. I was about to let out a relieved sigh and pat myself but the man of the house dropped his plate in the sink and walked away.

"Argh," I was tempted to shriek and pull my hair but I controlled my emotions as expressing my wrath wasn't considered to be professional.

After leaving every inch of the sink sparkling I began to sweep the floor. Picking up the toys strewn all over and chocolate wrappers hiding in every nook of the house I was trying my best to tidy the house.
Just then my eyes fell on a coffee mug hiding under the couch. I picked it up and the sight of the dried coffee marks got on my nerves.
"Argh," I let out a muffled shriek. It was important for me to vent you see.

After about thirty minutes, I was all set to begin my third task. Twirling the mop-stick in the bucket I began to mop the floor.

I had just finished mopping the living room leaving every bit of it shining. The lady of the house entered and began to walk on the wet floor pouring cold water over my efforts.
I stared at her with bloodshot eyes but she walked away nonchalantly.

I meticulously began to mop the floor all over again. What can I do? It was a part of my job.
Ahh, I was finally on the verge of reaching the finish line and calling it a day when I heard a voice.
"Did you fold the dried clothes?"

I knew that I hadn't signed up for it. But I have a bad habit. I can't say No and end up getting overworked.

Having no other option left I quickly folded the clothes and placed them on the table in the living room.

After taking leave from the mistress who didn't even look at me and just nodded, I walked out of the house. So what if I am a domestic help? I understand that I'm paid for my job but I have had my share of Argh moments. The insensitivity of people gets under my skin but I let go and continue doing my job. That's what we all do. Isn't it?
Let go and move on.

CHAPTER THIRTY-ONE

Can Her Soul Ever Heal?

Clasping a bag tightly, Veena sat staring at the students who were running around and filling the air with frolic. There was no sound like the undiluted laughter of the children. Tears surprised her, stinging her eyes. She had visited the campus a year back to enrol her son Varun. Emotions rose like waves. She let them flow freely without being a hindrance. Everything was rosy until a few days back. A fortnight back she had received a phone call from the administration. They informed her that Varun had drowned in the pool. She couldn't process the information back then. She had lost her child forever. She cursed herself for enrolling Varun in a boarding school. An employee handed her Varun's belongings and broke her reverie. She sat still dwelling in the memories. Can her soul ever heal? Only we can wish so.

CHAPTER THIRTY-TWO

Her Krishna

The aroma of the savouries wafted through the air filling the house with festivities. With the loose end of her saree tucked in her waist she began to make arrangements for the pooja. Suddenly, she heard mellifluous music. She walked to the door and her eyes fell on a boy dressed in ragged clothes. But the peacock feather on his head and the flute in his hand, cast their spell. She stood mesmerized, "Ask that vagrant to leave," said her mother-in-law sternly. She welcomed him inside and fed him. She believed that 'Service to mankind is service to God'.

CHAPTER THIRTY-THREE

Every Daughter's Wish

The moment I told you that I was feeling sick,
You let go of everything else and by my side did you stick,
The thermometer showed a rise in my body temperature giving you jitters,
You fed me with medicines bitter,
Everyone thought that it was the doctor's prescription that had nursed me back to good health,
But I know that it was your love that had done the magic,
Today though I'm a mother of two,
I miss you on days I feel sick,
Oh Mumma, why can't a daughter live under the protective umbrella of her mother forever?

CHAPTER THIRTY-FOUR

Dream Come True

As I enter the large and commodious aeroplane,
I travel down memory lane,
When I was a child,
I remember me running to the terrace on hearing the roar of an aeroplane,
The mere sight of it made my heart jump with joy,
Travelling by air became a part of my bucket list,
Today as I am seated comfortably in the cockpit,
I'm prepared to embrace my first air travel,
Travelling in the vast blue sky and taking a tour of the clouds is going to be pure bliss and
It will be etched in my memory forever.

CHAPTER THIRTY-FIVE

Facing The Consequences Of Comparison

Waking up at dawn, Shivani entered the kitchen. She had meticulously planned everything. Wanting to surprise her foodie husband she diligently prepared a wide range of delicacies. The aroma of the delectable food dragged her husband to the dining table, "Oh wow, sambar looks amazing," he remarked. "Did you like the breakfast?" asked Shivani expecting a compliment. "It was tasty. But it didn't taste as the sambar amma makes," he blurted. She stood in silence and he cursed himself for speaking his mind. He was prepared to face the storm. He is being served oats and cornflakes since then.

CHAPTER THIRTY-SIX

An Attempt To Restore Her Sanity

"Take a glance at his picture. I'm certain you will not say no," Sania's mother tried to convince her. "I'm looking for a svelte woman, I'm sorry," the suitor said haughtily that evening.

The same incident played on the loop, only the suitors were different. "Meet this boy," her glare interrupted her mother. "In the name of traditions I have been body-shamed myriad times. I'm imperfectly perfect and I don't seek a man's validation. I'm not a meek woman who's going to crush under judgements. There's more to me. I'm going on a detox man fast," she declared smiling confidently.

CHAPTER THIRTY-SEVEN

The Shining Puffy Delicacy

Adding water to the flour she kneaded the dough with precision. Rolling a portion of it, she dropped it in hot oil and waited with bated breath. The sight of the puffy, crisp pooris made her eyes twinkle with joy. 'Just the way they like it,' she thought. The family savoured the golden brown delicacy. She walked out of the kitchen drenched in sweat. "Mumma, I hate pooris," said her little one. "Why?" she asked perplexed. "The pooris are shining but soaked in sweat you have lost your sheen," he said. Lost for words, she hugged him tightly.

CHAPTER THIRTY-EIGHT

Jab Mile Teen Yaar

On the days I hit a low,
On the days I'm on the verge of beginning a tantrum throw,
On the days my mind is filled with tumult,
I take a panoramic view of my house,
'The chores have to wait,' I repeat to myself and
Sneak into my room for a therapeutic session with my besties,
Engulfed by silence and snuggled in my cosy bed,
As I unravel every leaf and dwell deeper in it,
I put my exasperation and angst to rest,
Solitude and books are my friends in need,
They help preserve my sanity indeed.

CHAPTER THIRTY-NINE

Fifty Fifty

The human mind is a powerhouse of intelligence. It is a reservoir of a plethora of emotions. Some of which are positive and the rest are negative. While the positive emotions like humanity, compassion and kindness reveal our angelic side, negative emotions like anger, greed and envy expose our monstrous disposition. We are all a combination of an angel and a monster. Strive to get rid of the virulent negative thoughts from time to time. Protect your mind with an antivirus called faith and optimism. Keep the monster at bay and Enjoy your life everyday.

CHAPTER FORTY

The Peak Of Clothes

After a long and exhausting day,
I ascended the stairs wearily,
Wiping the rivulets of sweat off my eyebrows,
I knocked on the door and
Prayed as I waited for the doorbell to be answered,
After a few seconds,
She opened the door and I greeted her,
My eyes began to scan every nook of the house,
It looked spic and span,
Crestfallen I diverted my gaze,
Just then clothes piled up in the laundry basket caught
my attention,
The peak of clothes gave me happiness,
After all, doing laundry was a chore for them but a
livelihood for me.

CHAPTER FORTY-ONE

Being Messy Is Okay

It's okay to have the furniture covered in dust,
If you have with you someone you can trust,
It's okay if the countertop is covered with grime,
If you get to spend with yourself some time,
The cobwebs on the walls will have to wait,
While magic with your words you create,
Let the dirt on the floor feel ignored,
Help your dreams and aspirations be restored,
It is okay if your house is messy,
If you live your life happy and sassy,
Also, take time to nurture your relationships,
As messy houses can be tidied but not messy
relationships.

CHAPTER FORTY-TWO

Celebrate Being A Girl Child

Carrying her carefully in her arms, Samhitha caught a closer glimpse of her baby. "We don't want a girl child. A daughter is a burden on the family," The heinous remarks of her family rang in her ears. Enveloping her daughter's hands in that of hers, 'My womb was supposed to be a haven for you. You faced every odd in those dreadful nine months, escaped foeticide and have emerged victorious. You are a warrior,' thought Samhitha. "I will name you Jhansi," she said. "Be fearless and celebrate being a girl child," said Samhitha and kissed her baby.

CHAPTER FORTY-THREE

My Favourite Moments

As I lay in the crib,
My eyes wide open,
I observe that you run across the house,
Taking care of everyone,
Always putting their needs above yours,
I eagerly wait for you to enter the room,
The sound of your anklets,
Fills me with delight,
Despite every bone of yours demanding rest,
You carry me in your arms and
Place me carefully on the bed,
Suddenly, I feel your soft hands massaging my body
with the aromatic oil,
This is my favourite time of the day Mumma,
When you and I get to spend some We Time together.

CHAPTER FORTY-FOUR

The Second Chance

The dried leaves rustled under Mitra's feet and A rasping wind gushed across her face. As she walked into the dilapidated mansion, she once called her home. She observed that the rapturous giggles and laughter were long gone and was replaced by ashes and burnt remains Lost in her thoughts, she stepped on a sheeny metal that lay on the floor. Picking it up she began to clean it. "Wheel of time" she read the words imprinted on the metal. As she continued to rub it, she was transported back in time, her eyes fell on her younger self dressed in pigtails. She was elated to find her parents. As they spent time together, suddenly, the house caught fire. Her mother tried to push Mitra out of the house. Through a small opening that was available, Mitra pushed her mother away and ran to the centre of the house, waiting to be enveloped by the fire. The Wheel Of Time had given her a second chance, to live with her parents and she didn't want to let go of it. If death would unite her with her parents, she decided so be it.

CHAPTER FORTY-FIVE

What Do We Deserve?

Whenever something bad happens,
We vehemently proclaim that we don't deserve this,
On the contrary when something good happens,
Why don't we ever ponder,
Do we deserve this?
Bad experiences coerce us to complain and lament,
But while revelling in the good happenings we forget the world around us,
Experiences irrespective of whether they are good or bad needs to be cherished,
As good experiences give us memories to hold on
While bad experiences teaches us lessons for life,
So the next time HE bestows us with events good or bad,
Let us bow our head, accept them and express our gratitude.

CHAPTER FORTY-SIX

Our Most Prized We Time

Strolling aimlessly on the busy roads,
Admiring the colourful earrings and bangles and
Buying the best amongst the lot,
Sipping the tea from a roadside stall,
We spoke about anything and everything under the sun,
Munching on the fried food we bared our souls,
We returned home at dusk not carrying multiple shopping bags in our hands but carrying a plethora of memories in our hearts,
My mother and I enjoyed every bit of our ladies day out,
We never indulged in extravagance,
But the moments we had spent together made it priceless,
I hope to recreate those moments again.

CHAPTER FORTY-SEVEN

Perspective Matters

Standing on the porch of his apartment on the first floor, Rivansh observed a bare naked young boy play in the scorching heat. The glistening marble balls caught his attention. 'I wish I could play like him but I'm locked in this cage,' he thought taking a panoramic view of his abode. The other boy looked up and his eyes fell on Rivansh. Rivansh's stylish clothes caught his attention. 'I wish I could live a comfortable life like him but here I am living a life gripped by poverty,' thought the other boy. Indeed, the other side is always greener.

CHAPTER FORTY-EIGHT

My Rendezvous With Him

His light brown skin made me feel passionate,
The inciting gaze of his attracted me like a magnet,
I coyly walked towards him,
With a heart filled with joy and hope to the brim,
Caressing his sheeny outside,
I was intrigued to unravel the mysteries he was holding deep inside,
The strong odour he emanated thrilled me,
I carefully began to flay every layer with glee,
Suddenly, my eyes began to feel watery,
Every inch of me was fiery,
As my knife penetrated deep into him,
I cried so much that day,
After all, chopping onions was no child's play.

CHAPTER FORTY-NINE

Live In The Present

Learn from your past mistakes,
But by dwelling in it never put your happiness at stake,
Be physically and emotionally present,
In the present moment,
Enjoy every second of it,
Fret not about the future,
It is just a mystery wrapped in a shimmery paper,
It will be unravelled in layers at the appropriate time,
But till then live in the present,
Understand its importance,
Because the present is a gift from God,
Thank HIM for it and
Don't let it slip through your fingers,
As time once lost cannot be regained.

CHAPTER FIFTY

Make Peace With Yourself

Let go of the resentments and troubles of the past,
Relinquish the negative thoughts over years your mind has amassed,
Stop grumbling about situations that have gone awry,
Don't whine about the opportunities that have gone dry,
Accept and embrace the circumstances you are in,
Express gratitude for every blessing you have been bestowed with,
Nurture your inner peace,
Only then every turmoil in your life would cease,
Remember, peace starts from within,
It's time we make peace with ourselves and
Make not just the International Day Of Peace but every day a day filled with peace.

CHAPTER FIFTY-ONE

An Empire Filled With Love

In a distant kingdom lived an indomitable king,
Who was in pursuit of a dauntless and kind-hearted prince,
For his intrepid and gracious daughter,
One morning when the king had gone hunting,
He came across a young man, whose face revealed a divine radiance,
The King fixated that the young man would be the heir to his empire,
Marriage happened amid the shower of flowers and blessings,
Declining the throne, the couple bid adieu,
Though the young man had no empire to call his own,
He treated his wife like a queen,
The couple formed their empire filled with love.

CHAPTER FIFTY-TWO

The Humble Pickle

As she strolled in the backyard oblivious of the midday heat,
"Post," The postman's voice broke her reverie,
She rushed outside and was greeted by a weary middle-aged man drenched in sweat,
Her mother's name on the letter lit up her face with a smile,
She thanked him and
He asked her if she could give him something to eat,
She served him curd rice and homemade pickle,
The curd rice soothed his senses,
The pickle tickled his taste buds and
The combination felt like heaven on earth,
Her mother's pickle recipe cast its spell one more time.

CHAPTER FIFTY-THREE

Better Late Than Never

Dear son and daughter,
Your mom and I had nurtured you for more than two decades,
We have foregone every desire of ours to fulfil your every whim,
We had reprimanded you for your actions myriad times,
We had laughed, cried and lived together,
You have now outgrown our laps and have developed wings of your own,
You have formed your own nest,
But remember that your elderly and weary parents are eagerly awaiting your arrival,
All we want is to spend a little time with you,
Ponder over it before it's too late.
Your's lovingly,
Mumma and Papa.

CHAPTER FIFTY-FOUR

Choose Hope - The Gift Of Miracles

Saadhana stood staring at him through the glass door while chanting the Mruthyunjaya mantra for the hundredth time. He lay on the bed battling for his life. Tubes and IV cannulas pierced through his frail body. Every day Saadhana woke up with a hope that he would open his eyes and recognize her but she ended up disappointed.

She observed that there was a slight change in his breathing pattern. The monitor showed a dip in his pulse. She stood trembling in fear trying to not let pessimistic thoughts enter her mind.

"Hope- The four-letter word that helps vanquish every fear, aids in the faster cure of a disease, banishes darkness and fills our life with light," she remembered the words she had spoken at a seminar three years back.

Through her misted eyes she observed that his breathing sank further. After a few minutes of struggle, he finally breathed his last. The person who had taught her to walk and talk, to dream and aspire, to stay hopeful, to fight against all odds and stand tall now lay lifeless.

The moment his heart stopped pumping, her breathing became irregular. She knew the truth but wasn't ready to accept it.

Suddenly, "Doctor," she shrieked and her voice echoed in the corridor.

After a few seconds, the doctor rushed inside.

"I'm sorry Dr Sadhana," he said patting her.

The word doctor rang in her ears. Watching her father suffer made her forget that she was a doctor herself. Despite knowing the fact that her father wouldn't survive she didn't want to give up.

All she had was her father. He was her sole support system. She couldn't imagine a life without him. She had treated innumerable patients in the past. She was a witness to both birth and death. She was a source of hope and motivation to her patients. She had helped them cope with loss.

"Once you choose hope, anything is possible," she said quoting Christopher Reeve.

But wasn't able to deal with her crisis.

Tears cascaded down her cheeks. Trying to pick up her bits and pieces, quivering like a leaf all the while she reached her home. She entered her father's room. The neatly folded bedspread, the study table in the corner with a pen stand, his books and documents arranged meticulously reminded her of him. She reminisced the late night coffee they had enjoyed together. She recollected the anecdotes he had shared with her. His aroma enveloped every inch of the room. She sank on the bed with her knees pulled close to her chest. Her eyes that were clouded with tears fell on a sheet of paper that lay under a diary.

She reached for it and began to read it.

Dear Saadhana,

When your mother had left this mortal world two decades back, I had lost the zeal to live. The world around me felt faded. I didn't want to continue living but you became the purpose of my life. My life began to revolve around you. Your happiness became my priority. You were the beacon of hope that chased away the darkness. It was when I realised the Power Of Hope. When I was diagnosed with cancer a month back I knew that I wouldn't survive. It will be difficult for you to cope with the loss but I don't want you to give up. Find your purpose. Save lives and express gratitude to HIM for every blessing he has bestowed you with. Do your duty, fulfil your responsibilities. Also, remember to smile. I will be alive in that pleasant smile of yours.

Take care, my princess.

Your's lovingly,
Papa.

Clasping the letter close to her chest, she began to weep profusely. The tears smudged the words in the letter. Life without her father would never be the same. But she had to move on. The power of hope will not allow her to give up.

As she lay on the bed drowning in myriad emotions, her phone rang.

"Dr Saadhana there's an emergency case. Can you please

attend to the patient?" spoke a nurse.
'Duty calling,' she thought and got off the bed. She was hopeful about saving that patient's life. Hope is indeed powerful. Isn't it?

Hope is the companion of power, the mother of success, for so who hopes strongly, has within him the gift of miracles.
- Samuel Smiles.

CHAPTER FIFTY-FIVE

The Truth Proved Costly To Her

Ignoring the dogs howling at a distance, Ritu entered the cabin located amid a dense jungle.

A lone bulb flickered in the corner. Leaving her bag on a mucky cot she sat on the floor.

It was a long and tiresome week at work and she hoped that this getaway destination would offer her respite.

Suddenly, the bulb went off. She reached for her phone and switched on the torch.

She closed her eyes and was about to doze off when she heard a series of footsteps.

The door opened with a creak and two men entered.

An hour later, her mother phoned her but her phone was out of reach.

Her phone lay deep inside the ground beside her lifeless body.

The news article she had written about a scam, revealing the names of powerful beauracrats had cost her her life.

CHAPTER FIFTY-SIX

Sinful Deeds And Its Consequences

A man with a beastly figure and distorted countenance sat on the throne.

"Hail the 'King Greed'," said another man who was standing with his head bent and hands folded.

He reached for a bag of coins and handed it to the guard, revealing his crippled arms.

The guard counted the coins and whispered something in the king's ears.

The king's eyes turned red and he reached for a sword. He was about to behead the man when the man fell to his knees and pleaded, "Please show some mercy.

We have been paying two hundred copper coins for Water, a hundred copper coins for Land and two hundred silver coins for Air.

Please don't increase the taxes lest the only option left is death.

The King smirked and clapped. A guard arrived holding a tray full of plastic.

The man was forcefully fed the plastic till he choked to death.

Mother Earth who was chained and held prisoner was in tears as she witnessed her child pay for his sins.

The sins that made Greed the king.

CHAPTER FIFTY-SEVEN

A Desire To Live

Having lived all life,
Striving to meet the expectations of all,
Her life has been nothing short of a strife,
In the pursuit of making others happy,
Her happiness was gone with the wind.
Struggling to fulfil the dreams and wishes of the rest,
Her dreams and aspirations were shoved under the carpet,
But the loss of a friend during the pandemic had come as an eye-opener to her.
She realised that death was just a breath away and she wasn't indispensable.
The moment of epiphany came as a game changer,
She decided to live life on her terms,
Without feeling an ounce of guilt.
Take her or leave her,
Love her or hate her.
She was sorry, but not sorry,
For she wanted to live and not just be alive.

CHAPTER FIFTY-EIGHT

No One Can Escape The Reality

The door opened and he entered.

He dragged a chair and sat in front of me.

He reached for a bottle and poured a few drops of its contents on cotton.

He carefully wiped his face. He looked deep into my eyes. He caressed his wrinkles.

The dark spots that were spread across his face, the dark circles that enveloped his eyes, grey eyebrows and crow's feet were revealed.

He looked at his 'real' self in disgust.

The make-up he applied every morning kept his glamour intact on the silver screen and helped in keeping the box office ringing.

He lived a lie all day but he couldn't escape from the reality whenever he looked at me, the mirror.

9 798887 046846

Printed by Libri Plureos GmbH in Hamburg, Germany